BEFORE YOU BEGIN...

Make sure to download the FREE audio program for this book which comes with your purchase! Just go to

www.slangman.com/audio

then look for your book and enter this code:

E2I2ZKUY3HDP

GOLDILOCKS and the 3 BEARS

Written by: David Burke
Copy Editor: Julie Bobrick
Illustrated by: "Migs!" Sandoval
Translator: Alessio Filippi
Proofreader: Valerio Morucci

Copyright © 2017 by David Burke

Email: info@heywordy.com
Website: www.heywordy.com

Hey Wordy! and all related characters and elements are © and trademarks of Hey Wordy, LLC.

Published by Slangman Publishing. Slangman is a registered trademark of David Burke. All rights reserved. Reproduction or translation of any part of this work beyond that permitted by section 107 or 108 of the 1976 United States Copyright Act without the permission of the copyright owner is unlawful. Requests for permission or further information should be addressed to the Permissions Department, Slangman Publishing. This publication is designed to provide accurate and authoritative information in regard to the subject matter covered. The persons, entities and events in this book are fictitious. Any similarities with actual persons or entities, past and present, are purely coincidental.

ISBN13: 978-1-891888-48-9

Printed in the U.S.A.

Meet the Author
David Burke

Creator and star of the children's TV show, *Hey Wordy!*, David Burke has been single-handedly revolutionizing the foreign language-learning movement worldwide.

In addition to being a performer of boundless energy and enthusiasm, David speaks seven languages. A successful author and entrepreneur, he has built a thriving international publishing company featuring over 100 books he has written for teen/adults & children. His books have won publishing awards and have sold more than one million copies. David's Street Speak™ and Biz Speak™ series of books and audio programs are used around the world by government agencies, leading universities and major corporations.

Since age 4, David has been a classically trained pianist and uses his musical gifts to compose and perform original songs for his TV series, *Hey Wordy!* which introduces children to foreign languages and cultures through music, animation, and magical adventures. He has also composed, orchestrated, and performed all the music in the audio programs for each of these books.

David's engaging and charismatic persona became a fixture on broadcast entertainment channels around the world, such as CNN and the BBC. David and his work have been highlighted in many major publications, including The Los Angeles Times, The Chicago Tribune and The Christian Science Monitor.

"This series teaches everyday words that occur in your child's life, as well as terms having to do with politeness, greetings, family & friendship."

David Burke

Italian vocabulary taught:

bambino = baby
caldo = hot
ciotola = bowl
cucina = kitchen
cuscino = cushion
due = two
duro = hard
freddo = cold
letto = bed
mamma = mama
morbido = soft

orso = bear
papà = papa
passeggiata = stroll
piccolo = little
poltrona = armchair
porta = door
stanca = tired
tavola = table
tre = three
uno = one

from Cindellera (Level 1)

arrivederci = goodbye
bella = pretty
bello = handsome
casa = house
cattiva = mean
felice = happy
festa = party
grande = big
grazie = thank you
innamorato = in love

mezzanotte = midnight
moglie = wife
momento = moment
piede = foot
prego = you're welcome
principe = prince
ragazza = girl
scarpa = shoe
triste = sad
vestito = dress

1

Once upon a time, there was a bear family who lived in a *grande casa* in the forest — a papa **orso**, a *bella* mama **orso**, and their pride and joy,

orso
papà
mamma

a little baby **orso**. The **piccolo bambino orso** was very *bello* like his **papà**. The **papà orso** was very much *innamorato* with the *bella* **mamma orso** and they were very

piccolo bambino

3

proud of their family. One day, the **bella mamma orso** prepared some soup for lunch, but it was too hot. While it cooled off, the **orso** family went for a stroll.

passeggiata

Meanwhile in a town nearby, there lived a **bella ragazza** named Goldilocks who was very *triste* because she was so tired of never having anything fun to do.

She thought for one **momento** and decided to take a **passeggiata** in the forest. Very soon, she came upon a **casa** and knocked on the [door] but no one

porta

was there. So she opened the **porta**, put one *piede* inside the *casa*, and said "Hello? Is anyone home?" She was very tired after her long **passeggiata** → **stanca**

tavola
cucina

and since no one answered, she walked inside the *casa*. She looked around for a *momento* and was very *felice* to see a *grande* table in the kitchen with food

on it! She quickly approached the *grande tavola* in the **cucina** and was super extra *felice* because there on the *grande tavola* in the **cucina** was a bowl — **ciotola**

uno
due
tre

but not just one, not just two, but three! **Uno, due, tre**! And the smell from each **ciotola** was wonderful! She took a taste from the *grande* **ciotola** of the **papà**

orso and said, "Oh! This is too hot !" → **caldo**
Then she took a taste from the **ciotola**
of the **mamma orso** and said, "Oh! This
is too cold !" Then she took a taste from → **freddo**

the **ciotola** of the **piccolo bambino orso** and said, "Ahhh. This one isn't too **caldo**. It isn't too **freddo**. It's just right!" And she ate everything in the **ciotola**. "*Grazie!*" she said

to the empty **ciotola**. Well, now she was even more **stanca** than ever after eating so much food. So, she stretched and stretched and decided to take a rest. In the living room,

poltrona ← she saw an armchair ...but not just **uno**, not just **due**, but **tre**! **Uno, due, tre**! So, she sat down in the *grande* **poltrona** and said,

cuscino ← "Oh! The cushion on this **poltrona** is too

hard!" So, she sat on the **cuscino** of the **poltrona** belonging to the **mamma orso** and said, "This **cuscino** is too soft!" Then she sat on the **cuscino** on the smallest

→ **duro**

→ **morbido**

poltrona and said, "This **cuscino** isn't too **duro**. It isn't too **morbido**. It's just right!" But at that very **momento**... CRACK! The **poltrona** completely fell apart!

Still **stanca**, she decided to look for the bedroom to take a **piccolo** nap. In front of her, she saw a bed, but not just **uno**, not just **due**, but **tre**!

letto

Uno, **due**, **tre**! So, she tried the *grande* **letto** of the **papà orso**, but it was too **duro**. Then she tried the **letto** of the **mamma orso** but it was too **morbido**. Finally, she tried the

piccolo letto and said, "Ahhh. This **letto** isn't too **duro**. It isn't too **morbido**. It's just right!" And she fell asleep. At that *momento*, the *grande* **papà orso**, the *bella* **mamma**

19

orso, and the **piccolo bambino orso** returned from their **passeggiata**. But the *grande* **papà orso** noticed something strange. "Someone's been eating my soup!"

said the **grande papà orso**. "And someone's been eating my soup!" said the **bella mamma orso**. "And someone's been eating MY soup and ate it all up!" cried the **piccolo**

bambino orso. "Look!" said the **grande papà orso**. "Someone's been sitting in my **grande poltrona**!" "And someone's been sitting in my **poltrona**!" said the

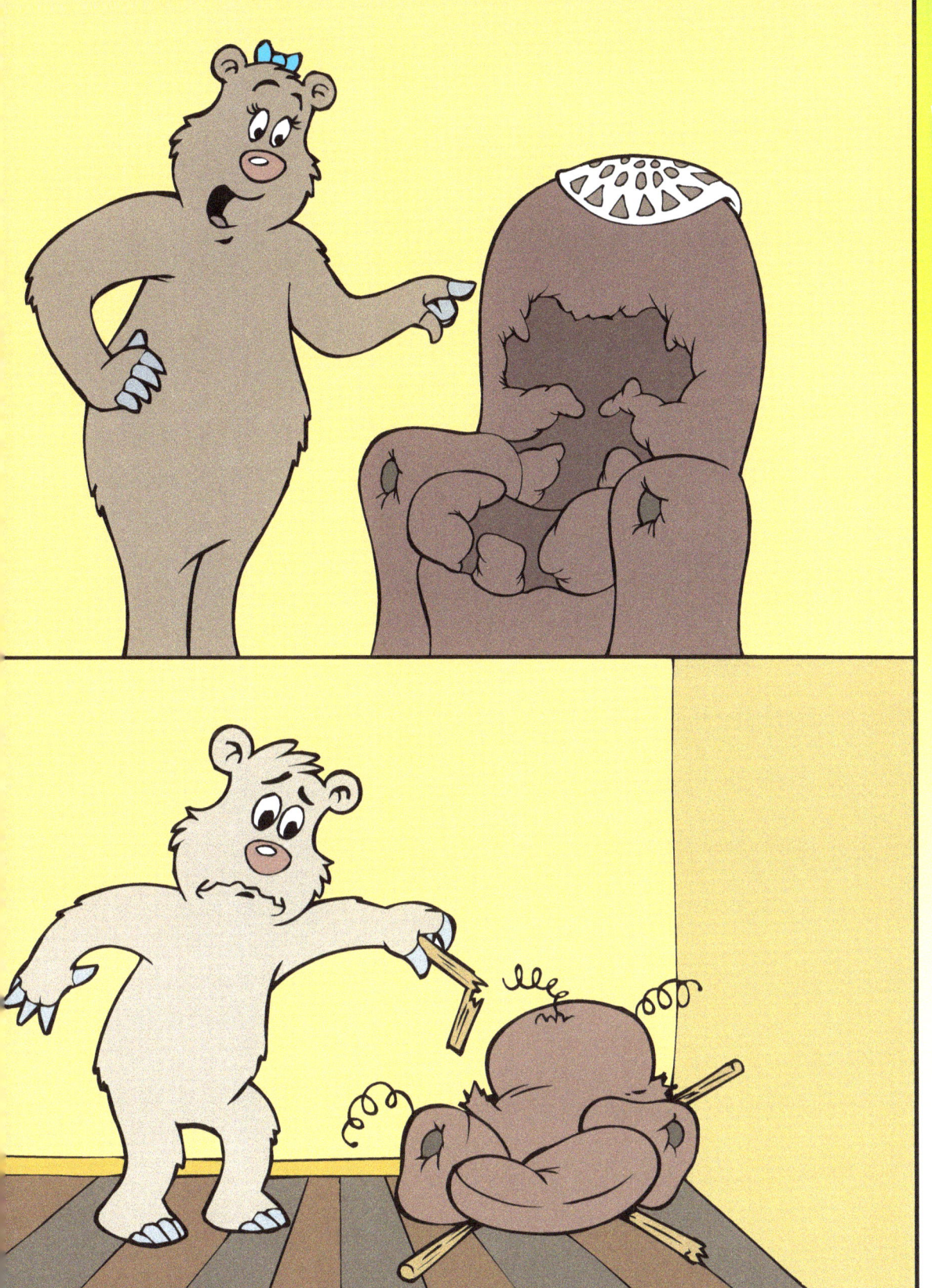

bella **mamma orso**. "And someone's been sitting in MY **poltrona** and broke it into pieces!" cried the **piccolo bambino orso**. Suddenly, the **orso** family heard

loud snoring coming from the bedroom, so they went in to look. "Someone's been sleeping in my **grande letto**!" said the **grande papà orso**. "And

someone's been sleeping in my **letto**!" said the **bella mamma orso**. "And someone's been sleeping in MY **piccolo letto** and there she is!" shouted the

piccolo bambino orso. Just then, Goldilocks woke up and saw the **orso** family! Well, they thought that the *ragazza* was very *cattiva* to use their *casa* without

permission! "Oh, *grazie!*" she said to the **papà orso**. "*Grazie* for letting me eat food from your **ciotola**, sit in your **poltrona**, and lie in your **letto**!" Goldiocks said "*Grazie!*"

again expecting the **orso** family to say, "*Prego!*" but they were angry that she caused so much trouble in their *casa* and the **orso** family growled at her.

So, she slowly stood up on the **letto** of the **piccolo bambino orso**, and nervously said, "Well, **grazie** for having me and... **Arrivederci**!" And with that, Goldilocks

29

jumped off the **piccolo letto**, and dashed out the front **porta**, running as fast as each **piede** could move. Needless to say, she never returned to the **casa** of the **orso** family again.

Now you're ready for Level 3!

Level 3 contains words from Levels 1 & 2, plus all NEW words!

For more HEY WORDY! products, visit...

www.HEYWORDY!.com

www.ingramcontent.com/pod-product-compliance
Lightning Source LLC
Chambersburg PA
CBHW042031100526
44587CB00029B/4377